Dogs With Jobs

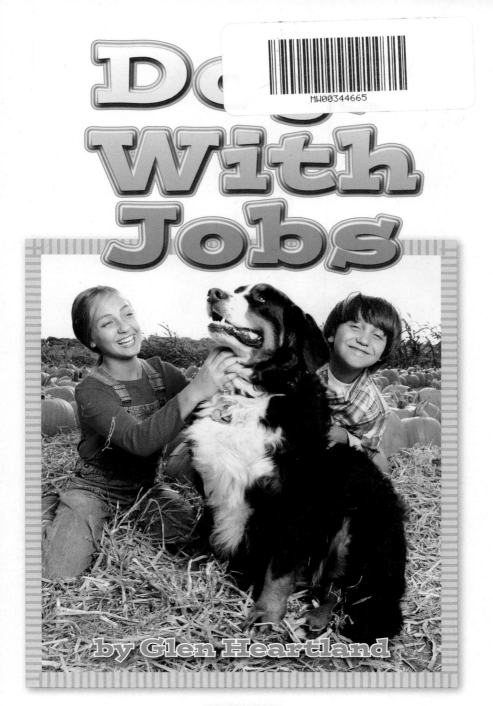

by Glen Heartland

PEARSON

Glenview, Illinois • Boston, Massachusetts • Chandler, Arizona
Upper Saddle River, New Jersey

Man's best friend.

Dogs are often called "man's best friend." People and dogs have lived together for thousands of years. Today most dogs are pets. Their "job" is to be a good friend to their owner.

But there are also many working dogs. These dogs are trained to help people.

What does the dog smell?

Dogs have an amazing sense of smell. This talent has made dogs very helpful to humans. For example, dogs can smell much better than we can. They can smell about 1,000 times better!

They can smell "cold," or old, scents. Suppose you drop a sandwich on the sidewalk. Dogs can smell it days later!

---

scents: smells

When a dog sniffs, it rapidly breathes in and out of its nose. This helps the dog smell better. Dogs sniff odors in the air and on the ground. Some dogs can smell things several miles away.

People train dogs to smell different things. They can smell things we cannot such as fruits or other animals.

A dog sniffs the ground.

rapidly: quickly
odors: smells

People use dogs to find and rescue people. They have done this for hundreds of years.

A Saint Bernard is a large dog that is famous for rescuing people. They are used in the vast mountains of Switzerland. Saint Bernards can find people buried in the snow. They lick people's faces to keep them awake. They lie down beside them to keep them warm.

Saint Bernards are rescue dogs.

---

rescue: save
beside: next to

Dogs have also helped farmers for thousands of years. The first job dogs ever had may have been guarding animals. Today, some dogs are raised to live in the fields with farm animals. They are very gentle with the animals. But they will attack to keep the animals safe.

Dogs guard farm animals.

---

raised: brought up, taught from an early age

Other dogs are trained to herd animals, or keep them together. They move them from one place to another. They bring back animals that have roamed away.

Sometimes owners cannot be with their dogs. The dogs must work with the animals on their own. They must be able to do their jobs by themselves.

Herding sheep.

Herding dogs work in cities and suburbs, too. Geese travel in large groups. They like to visit places with lots of grass, such as golf courses and parks. Geese can hurt the grass. They often get in the way of people playing.

Herding dogs are trained to chase away the geese.

Herding geese.

You know that farm dogs guard animals in the fields. But they can also do many other jobs. They can bring in cows and chickens at night. They can find lost animals. They can watch over children as they play. They can keep pigs and goats out of the family garden.

A good farm dog is a great helper for a farmer.

Farm dogs do many jobs.

Some dogs are called "service dogs." They help their owners live normal lives. Seeing eye dogs, for example, guide blind people. Their jobs are very important. It is not a good idea to pet or talk to a seeing eye dog. The dog must pay attention to his or her job.

Seeing eye dogs guide their owners

service: helpful act

Hearing ear dogs are another kind of service dog. They alert deaf people to important sounds, such as a phone or a car horn.

Service dogs are with their owners all the time. They can go in places that do not allow dogs. They can go into schools and restaurants. These dogs are very well behaved. They want to do their jobs well.

Hearing ear dogs help deaf people.

alert: warn

The first dogs probably had important jobs. They helped people live safer, easier lives. Today, many dogs have special jobs. They help us do things we cannot do by ourselves.

Pet dogs have important jobs, too. They give us love and friendship. They make us feel safe. And they make us happy! A good dog is a great friend.

Dogs with jobs.